organise

Please return or renew this item before the latest date shown below

10·15

INVERKEITHING

15 APR 2022

10 SEP 2022

WITHDRAWN FROM STOCK

05

- 6 JUN 2016

17 SEP 2016

2 0 OCT 2016

28 JUN 2017

27/7/17

12 APR 2018

3 0 MAY 2018

12 JUL 2018

Thank you for using your library

First published in 2013 by Wrightbooks

an imprint of John Wiley & Sons Australia, Ltd

42 McDougall St, Milton Qld 4064

Office also in Melbourne

Typeset in ITC Berkeley Oldstyle Std Book 11/13.5

Organise Your Home © MaryAnne Bennie 2013

Excerpts taken from *From Stuffed to Sorted*, first published in 2012 by John Wiley & Sons Australia, Ltd

The moral rights of the author have been asserted

National Library of Australia Cataloguing-in-Publication data:

Author:	Bennie, MaryAnne.
Title:	Organise your home: de-clutter, de-stress / MaryAnne Bennie.
ISBN:	9781118626559 (pbk.)
	9781118678718 (ebook)
Subjects:	Housekeeping.
	House cleaning.
	Home economics.
Dewey Number:	640.41

Illustrations: © Tom Wilson

Cover design by Susan Olinsky

Cover image: © iStockphoto.com/Caner Tan Bidci

Internal design by Peter Reardon, www.pipelinedesign.com.au

Printed in Singapore by C.O.S. Printers Pte Ltd

10 9 8 7 6 5 4 3 2

Disclaimer

Contents

About the author　　　　　　　　　　　　　　　　　　　　　*iv*

Introduction　　　　　　　　　　　　　　　　　　　　　　　*v*

1　Masterclass 1: setting up for success　　　　　　　　　　　1

2　Masterclass 2: the in8steps system　　　　　　　　　　　　8

3　Masterclass 3: a space mission　　　　　　　　　　　　　　32

4　Masterclass 4: getting a handle on hardware　　　　　　　　37

5　Masterclass 5: time-saving techniques　　　　　　　　　　　55

6　Bedroom boost　　　　　　　　　　　　　　　　　　　　　61

7　Fresh faces for living spaces　　　　　　　　　　　　　　　78

About the author

MaryAnne Bennie is Australia's organising guru. She began her professional organising career after realising that being organised was one of the most valuable, transferrable life skills a person could possess.

In this book, MaryAnne introduces readers to the in8steps system and shows how easy it is to apply these steps to totally reorganise the stuff in your life and turn houses back into homes. As a wife, mother and businesswoman, MaryAnne fully understands the struggle to juggle home, office and life. The in8steps system is tried and tested and, if followed, will work for everyone regardless of how much stuff or space they have.

Prior to becoming a professional organiser, MaryAnne was a senior lecturer at a leading Australian university. She holds a Bachelor of Education and Master of Business.

MaryAnne's organising expertise is regularly featured in newspapers and magazines, and on websites and radio. She motivates and inspires people, and fully equips them with the information and tools they need to organise their homes, their offices and their lives.

Introduction

Well begun is half done.

Aristotle

Regardless of where we live or what we do, we acquire and accumulate items meant to enhance our quality of life. We call these items our possessions, our assets, our things or our stuff. These items come in the form of furniture, clothing, entertainment equipment, tools, cookware, crockery, cutlery, supplies, food, glassware, ornaments, artwork, books, transport, technology, appliances, footwear, paperwork, sports equipment and toys. And that just names a few! When in balance, these items are useful and appreciated: they support us in our endeavours and make life easier and more comfortable.

We have an infinite capacity to bring stuff in, but we have a finite capacity to store our stuff. *Everything is competing for space.* Everything needs to earn its right to stay! When something doesn't have a home, it's homeless. Because homeless items have nowhere specific to live, they live anywhere and everywhere. They line the hallways, park on benches, slide under beds, perch on cupboard tops and hide in corners. Then they breed like rabbits! Before we know it we have a house full of mess and the resulting chaos has a detrimental impact on our quality of life.

We think more storage will solve the problem so we add cupboards, shelving and containers. Some of us renovate or put on an extension; others relegate the car into the driveway or the street and use the garage as a storage solution. When desperate, we may resort to the 'out-of-sight, out-of-mind' storage technique and rent off-site storage to deal with the excess. If only we had a bigger house, everything would be fine!

Our possessions should support us and our lifestyle. They should reflect our personality and style. They should bring us happiness, not despair. Why, then, do we find the things we took so much pleasure in acquiring are now suffocating us, causing us misery and wasting our precious time?

Sadly, some of the things we acquired on past shopping expeditions no longer have their magnetic appeal. Our love affair is over!

The in8steps system helps you to reassess your relationship with your stuff. It shows you how to decide what stays and what goes, and how to efficiently store what remains so it's ready and available when you need it. The delicate balance between your stuff and your available storage is restored. In this new relationship, your stuff will support you now and into the future. But when the time comes to part company, you will know how to gently break the news. The in8steps system will show you the way.

So climb on board. Ready or not, here we go!

Chapter 1

Masterclass 1: setting up for success

Vision without action is merely a dream.
Action without vision just passes the time.
Vision with action can change the world!

Joel Arthur Barker

In the mood

Remember the last time you went on a trip? You did some planning, chose a destination, set the dates, decided how to get there, booked your accommodation and set aside some spending money. You really got in the mood. You imagined being in new places, meeting new people and having new experiences. That's how I want you to feel about this trip to your new destination of being organised. I want you to see, feel, smell, hear and taste it. I want the excitement of it to be pulsing through your veins throughout your journey.

Complete the following three exercises to get you in the ultimate organising mood.

Exercise 1: be organised

What does being organised mean to you? Is it having a place for everything and everything in its place? Is it not being embarrassed if someone pops in? Is it having time to do all the things you have been putting on hold all these years?

Visualise it!

Imagine you had a crystal ball and you could see your organised future. What would you see, smell, feel, taste and hear? Take a few moments to visualise and experience your organised future through your crystal ball. Visualise every room in your home in its organised state and ask yourself these questions:

✓ What do I see?

✓ How does it smell?

✓ What can I feel?

✓ How does it taste?

✓ What can I hear?

Now close your eyes and answer the questions.

Write your responses for each room in your notebook.

Exercise 2: calculate your savings
No time to waste!

How much time and money will you save by being more organised?

You already know that being disorganised costs time and money. But have you ever really thought about how much time and money you will save? Being more organised streamlines every single thing you do: from getting ready in the morning, to going to work, to making dinner, to looking after the house, to retiring in the evening. If you're disorganised, every single thing you do takes more time than necessary. It could be the few extra minutes it takes to move the junk off the ironing board to iron a shirt for work, or the time you waste every day looking for wallets, purses, glasses, remote controls and keys. Maybe it's the 30 minutes you spent on hold on the phone, waiting to explain why you shouldn't have your power cut off, after forgetting to pay the misplaced bill.

Now let's look at your situation and time it.

Tick, tock! Time it!

Calculate your time saving: just think back over the past week and note the time you wasted through being disorganised. The amount of time you wasted will become the amount of time you save.

I will gain _____ hours a week by being more organised. My time savings will come from:

_____

Money down the drain!

When it comes to money, just think about the food you waste every week simply because you have no idea what you need when you go shopping. What about the things you buy again because you can't find the ones you already have? If you have ever wasted money on late fees, interest charges and fines for being tardy with your bills, you know how much that hurts. Is your car fading in the sun and losing value due to a disorganised garage? What about other frustrating things such as lost gift vouchers and receipts for warranty items needing repair?

Now let's look at your situation and cost it.

K-ching, k-ching! Cost it!

Calculate your money saving: just think back over the past week and calculate what you lost through being disorganised. The amount of money you lost will become the amount of money you save.

I will save $_____ a week by being more organised. My money savings will come from:
_____

Now let's look at your situation and spend it.

Spend it!

You have calculated how much time and how much money you will save by being organised. Now look into the future and imagine how you will spend that time and money.

How will you spend the extra time you have and extra money you save? _____

Exercise 3: shift your thinking
Talk to yourself!
It's now time to change your mindset.

So often it's the things you say to yourself that keep you from moving forward. This inner conversation is called self-talk. The good thing is that every negative statement you say about yourself or your situation can be turned around to be more positive. Statements such as, 'I've always been disorganised' are not helpful to your success. Instead say, 'I'm learning new organisation skills to achieve my goals'. From now on, focus on the future and forgive the past. Make positive statements every time you slip into negative thinking by changing your self-talk.

Change your mind! One of the self-talk changes you can make is to change from the old idea of 'letting go' to the new concept of 'releasing'. Many people find it hard to 'let go' of their stuff. 'Letting go' assumes a tug of war, with you holding on against an enemy who is pulling your stuff away from you. Well, you don't have to 'let go' of anything. You get to choose what stays and what goes. Your goal is to 'release' items that no longer serve or support you. This simple mindset change frees you to 'release' your things onto the next phase of their journey. It's not all about you. The stuff you 'release' has a higher purpose and a new place to be, serving people who have different needs from you.

Re-frame it!

Make a list of your negative self-talk statements and turn them into new, positive ones. Here is an example to start you off on a more positive note.

Negative self-talk	Positive self-talk
I don't have time to get organised.	I can break it down and do a little bit at a time.

Marcia's moving on

Marcia was moving house and she told me something that stuck with me. As she was packing, she asked herself a simple question: 'What things do I want to accompany me into the next phase of my life? What items have earned the right to continue to be in my new space and in my new life?' The items she loved and needed and those from which she received support were packed, while the rest were sent on their own journey elsewhere.

The key is to focus on what you are 'keeping' and not on what you are 'releasing'.

Whether you are moving into a new home or simply reorganising your existing home — affectionately known as 'moving without moving' — the process is the same. From now on you have the opportunity to make a conscious decision about every single item you possess. You have the chance to make a fresh start with a clean slate.

Now that your mood and confidence have been lifted, you are ready to learn the in8steps system. So read on.

The in8steps system

initi8	Start the process, and set your vision and goals.
investig8	Take a good look around to see what you have.
consolid8	Bring like items together.
elimin8	Release what you don't need, use, want or love.
alloc8	Allocate containers and space for what you are keeping.
activ8	Put things into their new locations.
evalu8	Check how it's working.
celebr8	Maintain the system and celebrate your success.

Chapter 2

Masterclass 2: the in8steps system

Your life is the sum result of all the choices you make, both consciously and unconsciously. If you can control the process of choosing, you can take control of all aspects of your life. You can find the freedom that comes from being in charge of yourself.

Robert F. Bennett

Learning the ropes

Remember when you first learned to drive a car? You had to figure out how all the parts of the car worked separately. You practised using the brakes, the accelerator and the steering. You started off having to concentrate on every step, one at a time: 'Put seatbelt on. Start car. Check mirrors. Indicate intentions. Drive forward.' Then, all of a sudden, it all came together and you were driving on a busy street. Learning the in8steps system is no different. Once you learn the steps, the system will come together automatically.

Phase it in

The in8steps system provides you with easy-to-follow instructions to support you through any organisation project:

 The first two steps are the 'Plan it' phase—for planning and preparation before you begin.

 The next four steps are the 'Do it' phase, where the actions of physical sorting and storing are done.

 The final two steps are the 'Review it' phase—for evaluation, maintenance and celebration.

One step at a time

I will show you how to do each step separately, how each phase comes together as a set and how to fast-track the system. So take the time to read through and understand the steps, as your results will be a reflection of how well you follow them.

The in8steps system in a nutshell

Here's a clear breakdown of the three phases and eight steps of the in8steps system in table 2.1 (overleaf).

Table 2.1: the in8steps system

Plan it	1 initi8	You initiate a plan of attack for your organising project.
	2 investig8	You investigate what you have and how it's working.
Do it	3 consolid8	You consolidate what you have into categories.
	4 elimin8	You eliminate things you no longer use, need, want or love.
	5 alloc8	You allocate space and containers for what you are keeping.
	6 activ8	You activate by preparing space, adjusting storage and placing items into their locations.
Review it	7 evalu8	You evaluate how it looks and works and make adjustments.
	8 celebr8	You celebrate by setting up maintenance and rewarding your success.

The in8steps system is common sense, easy to follow and guaranteed to work for your situation. Once you have mastered the theory, you will be ready to put it into practice in any area of your home. So get your notebook out—we're ready to go!

The in8steps system in detail

Let's look at each of the eight steps, one by one.

 ## Step 1: initi8

The first of the two planning steps is initi8. It will start you on your journey to an organised home. It's like turning on the ignition switch in your head but, as you know, turning on an ignition switch doesn't actually get you moving forward. You need to apply the accelerator and fully commit yourself to the task.

To travel along the correct route you need to identify your frequent frustrations, set your vision and your goals, gather your tools and get in the mood. This won't take long, so hop in the driver's seat and let's get started.

Identify your frequent frustrations

After choosing the room to be organised, you will list everything that frustrates you about it. What annoys you and constantly gets on your nerves? You need to feel the pain in order to appreciate the gain! Get it all down on paper because your frequent frustrations will lead you to your goals. Most of your frequent frustrations will be small things repeated over and over again. So make sure you list things such as running out of underwear, finding wet towels on the bed, jumbling through the entire plastics drawer and not finding what you want, tripping over toys or not knowing what's for dinner at night.

Set your vision and your goals

Keeping your frequent frustrations in mind, write your vision and your goals for each room. Remember: you will be measuring your success against the vision and the goals you set. In your vision and goals statement make sure you include what you want to achieve, an estimated budget, your timeline and a reward for completion.

Pamela's pantry plan

Pamela's simple vision and goals statement for her pantry was 'My pantry is filled with fresh, nutritious food for my family. Extra shelves have been installed to reduce space wastage and I now have a great system for managing my spices. I have two drawers filled with see-through containers holding all the staples I use every day. Everything is labelled and easy to remove, use and replace. I am allowing all day Tuesday and $500 to get it right. Once it's finished I'll treat myself to a massage and a facial'.

Gather your tools

You'll need to assemble an organising kit, a tool kit and a cleaning kit to assist you in this process.

The organising kit is everything you need in order to do your sorting. In particular, you will be using a number of temporary sorting containers during the process. Make do with what is available around the home such as cardboard boxes, shoe boxes, plastic containers of all sizes, bowls, cups, buckets, trays and so on. You should also collect empty boxes from the local supermarket or liquor store. A container is simply a receptacle or an area for gathering like items together. Tabletops, bench surfaces, floors and tops of beds should also be used for sorting. So you might place all your glassware onto a table or benchtop when sorting the kitchen, or place stacks of clothing onto the bed as you tackle the wardrobe. The organising kit also contains your notebook and pen, a camera and your sorting accessories.

The tool kit is essential for when you need to tighten a screw, adjust a shelf or repair a hinge. Keep it handy and in a designated spot (for example, just outside the door of the room you are working in). Most likely you already have a tool kit in the garage or workshop.

The cleaning kit will be used to spot clean along the way and to thoroughly clean storage surfaces before replacing your sorted items. It is easily made up with items you have in the house. See table 2.2 for a list of the kits you will need.

Table 2.2: your kits

Organising kit	Tool kit	Cleaning kit
Notebook and pen	Tape measure	Duster
'Bin it', 'Gift it', 'Sell it', 'Move it' containers	Hammer	Bucket with clean soapy water
Range of sorting containers	Screwdrivers	Sponges
Masking tape and marking pen	Pliers	Cleaning cloths
Label maker and tape	Spanners	Gloves
Garbage bags	Scissors	Apron
Zip-lock bags	Step ladder	Floor cleaners
Rubber bands	Packing Tape	Dust mask
Timer	Drill	Cleaning sprays
Camera	Extension cords	Surface protection cloths

Get in the mood

Before you begin organising, get into the right frame of mind for the task ahead. Here are several suggestions for keeping you focused and on track:

- Work with music playing, turn it up and move to the beat!

- Have lots of water and a few healthy snacks on hand.

- Divert your phones to message bank. This is no time to take calls.

- Turn your TV and computer off—emails can wait.

- Get the family out of the house unless they are actively involved in what you are doing.

- Dress for success. Wear comfortable clothes and shoes.

(Plan it) Step 2: investig8

The second planning step is investig8 and your role is to look at your room from an objective perspective, as though seeing it for the very first time.

Before you tackle any room, take a few minutes to look around and assess the space. Doing this now will save you making annoying mistakes later, such as finding that you have placed something needing power too far away from a power point. Or having glare from a window shining onto your computer screen. Or finding you have placed things in the wrong location. During the investig8 step you should do five quick things:

- *Carry out an overview.* Note the physical, functional and emotional elements of the room. Put simply, physical covers all the tangible items in the room, functional covers all the tasks performed in the room and emotional is all about how the room makes you feel. These three space elements are covered in detail in masterclass 3.

- *Measure up.* If you feel you need to play around with the furniture and storage components, draw a floor plan and take measurements as necessary. Not all rooms will require alteration, but be ready to make any changes that will address your frequent frustrations and achieve your vision and your goals. In particular, you may need to measure shelves and drawers to work out the best possible storage solutions.

- *Take unhappy snaps.* Take photos of each room and the insides of cupboards and drawers. Be careful—items sometimes have a habit of tumbling out when you least expect it! These 'before' photos will be fascinating to look back on once your organising is complete and they will also motivate you to stay on track.

- *Complete a discovery tour.* Look in every cupboard, drawer, nook and cranny to see what is stored there. You will discover lots of interesting stuff during your inspection, so be prepared to hear yourself repeating, 'Oh, that's where it is!' every time you discover some long lost item from your 'Where did I put it?' list. This inspection gives you a good idea of which items are stored where and it will be invaluable when you begin sorting your stuff into categories later on. It also reveals storage potential because you will discover that some cupboards and drawers are mainly filled with junk. All of a sudden, after ditching the junk, you will have bonus storage you didn't know about.

- *Fix anything that needs fixing.* Note anything you need to purchase or fix in your notebook. You may notice hanging hinges, loose handles, dripping taps, wonky drawers, blown light bulbs or sagging shelves. By noting them now, you can quickly rectify problems yourself or have plenty of time to call in professional help if required.

Your two planning and preparation steps are now complete and it's time to get into action.

 Step 3: consolid8

Consolid8 is the first of the four action steps. These action steps — consolid8, elimin8, alloc8 and activ8 — work together as a team, so as soon you begin consolidating a category — for example, 'linen' — you begin to involve the next three steps. This will become obvious as you read on.

Big fat categories

The consolid8 step shows you how to sort your stuff into big fat categories without turning the house upside down. A 'big fat category' is a broad category used to group a collection of like items together. The broadness of the category depends on the quantity, disarray and variety of what you are sorting. Big fat categories can easily be sorted into subcategories. For example, the big fat category of 'linen' can be sorted into the subcategories of sheets, towels, pillowcases, tea towels, tablecloths and so on.

The fab four

Eliminating stuff is the holy grail of organising! To get a room organised it's essential that we reduce the amount of stuff in it, and there are four ways of achieving this. You can 'Bin it', 'Gift it', 'Sell it' or 'Move it'.

You will need four rigid containers to house these categories. Put a label on each container and they are ready to accompany you on your organising mission. Take them with you on every organising job and try to fill them as much as possible! Here's what you fill them with:

- The 'Bin it' container is for obvious rubbish, including rubbish for recycling, and for unwanted items of no commercial value or use to anyone else.

- The 'Gift it' container is for stuff you no longer want but which is of some commercial value and is of use to someone else. You can gift it to family, friends or charity.

- The 'Sell it' container is for stuff you no longer want, but which has significant commercial value. It can be sold online or in a garage or yard sale. Of course, if you don't plan to sell your unwanted stuff you won't need this container.

- The 'Move it' container is for stuff you still want, but which does not belong in this room. Place items you plan to repair into this container as well.

Many items will go instinctively into these four containers during the consolidate step. As you can see, you are already integrating the elimin8 step into this earlier consolid8 step.

Tip

Label all your sorting containers using masking tape, which can be easily removed later but won't fall off like sticky notes or pieces of paper.

Sally sorts her baby's room

Sally gives her old—but good—baby clothes, toys and equipment to her sister Rebecca and recycles the rest. She doesn't have the time or energy to sell her stuff so she doesn't need a 'Sell it' bin. So when sorting the baby's room, she grabs some cardboard boxes and first creates a 'Rebecca' box and a 'recycle' box. Her grandmother does all her clothing repairs and so the 'Nana' box is born. As the boxes fill—or at the end of her organising—she places them into her car, ready to be delivered to their relevant destinations.

Remember that what you call your containers needs to make sense to you. Sally's made perfect sense to her.

Don't mess it up

When organising a room, you are faced with the prospect of making a huge mess in the process. The last thing you should do is take everything out at once—you simply won't have anywhere to put it all. And if you had to stop for any reason, you would be in a worse mess than you were to start with!

Steady as you go

Take it easy, work systematically and tackle one area or one category at a time, to keep the task manageable. For example, in the kitchen you could tackle the 'pantry' as an area or 'pots and pans' as a category. The pantry could be subcategorised into cans, cereals, dry goods, crackers and biscuits, spices, sauces and so on. The 'pots and pans' could be put into the subcategories of frypans, small pots, medium pots and large pots.

Work with what you have

Big fat categories are a starting point designed to bring like items together so you can deal with them as a group. This keeps the number of sorting containers you need to start with to a minimum. If, however, you are only sorting your linen cupboard, then everything in the cupboard is already sorted into the big fat category of 'linen'. You would immediately sort into subcategories such as towels, tea towels, beach towels, sheets, tablecloths and so on. Most of your storage will already be somewhat sorted into categories, so use this to your advantage. You can also rearrange things within the storage instead of taking everything out. You will still need sorting containers to consolidate items that don't belong. While you are doing this, you are also eliminating unwanted items to the 'Bin it', 'Gift it', 'Sell it' and 'Move it' containers.

Disaster zone!

If you have a room that is a total disaster, where stuff is piled and spread haphazardly around the room, you will need to create the biggest, fattest categories you can. For example, 'clothing' would be placed into one container (or one corner of the room), 'toys and games' into another, 'reading material' into another and so on. These would then be broken down into subcategories once the first sort has been completed. The four constant categories—'Bin it', 'Gift it', 'Sell it' and 'Move it'—will have significantly reduced the amount of stuff remaining, making it much easier to sort each big fat category into its subcategories one at a time.

Worst first

If you are working in a room that already has most of its contents stored in reasonable categories, work with these categories and areas last. First, tackle the areas that are in disarray (such as the junk cupboard) using big fat categories to group like items together. Once the junk cupboard is empty, place as many as you can of your big fat category containers back into the cupboard to get them out of the way temporarily. Now choose the next area to sort and integrate items into the existing big fat categories in the cupboard and create new ones as necessary. As soon as you know one big fat category is complete, you can move that category on to the next step: elimin8.

Kate's corner conquered

When Kate was organising her pots and pans, she removed them from their drawers and eliminated those she no longer wanted. After considering all her space, she decided she wanted to use the corner cupboard for her pots and pans, but it was overflowing with an assortment of plastic containers. As her plastic containers were already in their big fat 'plastic containers' category, she decided to take them straight to her sorting table where she first matched all the lids with the bases and tossed the leftover lids. She decided that she would only keep the plastic containers that stacked easily and neatly together and tossed those that did not meet her criteria. Now she could see what she had left. She placed them into two containers and decided to store them on a shelf of another cupboard. But this was full of cookbooks, which became the next category she had to deal with. And so it continued.

Some order please!

The sequence in which you sort your categories will often be self-determining. When you take items out of one location, sometimes they are returned to the same spot, while at other times they are best stored elsewhere. In order to store them elsewhere, you need to remove the things that are already there. So whatever was stored there determines the next area and categories you tackle. And so it continues. If items are put back in the same location, you get to choose the next area and categories you want to organise.

Fast forward!

Within a short time you will have consolidated all your categories and broken them down into subcategories, and maybe for the first time you will see just how much you have. The consolid8 step leads directly into the elimin8 step. Remember: you don't have to have consolidated everything to move to this step. As soon as you are pretty sure you have any category fully consolidated into subcategories, you can move forward to the next step and start eliminating.

 # Step 4: elimin8

Elimin8 is the second of the four action steps. This step finally and completely gets rid of what you don't use, need, want or love and sets some limits for the future. To proceed to this step you must have at least one category fully sorted into its subcategories. For example, 'linen' will have been sorted into towels, tea towels, beach towels and so on. Much of what you started with has already been discarded along the way because they were easy decisions. If you have linen stored in other areas of the house, collect it now and sort it into the subcategories as well. You can now see exactly how much of each subcategory you have, and how much space it will need. This is very valuable information and it may be the first time you have seen all these items together in the one place. You may be shocked by the amount you see!

Right size?

If you are really serious about getting organised, it is essential that you reduce the amount of stuff you keep to the things you use, need, want or love. Do you remember the 80:20 rule? A whopping 80 per cent of your stuff is used irregularly or not at all! Your aim is not to downsize for downsizing's sake, but to 'right size' for your current and future needs.

It's crunch time

Do a final sort of your subcategories to see what can go into the 'Bin it', 'Gift it', 'Sell it' or 'Move it' containers—and be ruthless! If you are having difficulty deciding, you are not alone. Everyone struggles to some extent with releasing some items. When in serious doubt, place the item into a container labelled 'Not sure' and keep moving through your subcategories. Finally, go back to your 'Not sure' container and ask yourself the following questions while holding each item:

- Do I use you? If so, how often? When was the last time? When will be the next time?

- Do I need you? Could I use something else as a substitute or borrow you?

- Do I really want you or just the memory of you or where you came from? If you just want the memory, take a photo!

- Do I love you? Are you of sufficient sentimental value for me to keep?

From the answers you give to these four questions, you will know whether to keep or to release the item.

Home shopping—your household supermarket

Create a family household supermarket for extra supplies of commonly used items. This secondary storage space can be in the garage, in a hall cupboard or in the laundry. Store extra toilet paper, tissues, shampoo, toothpaste, soap, washing detergent, sponges and those items you are lucky enough to buy at special prices. Whenever you run out of these in primary storage, go shopping in your household supermarket. Having a household supermarket reduces the stress on your primary storage space.

Only love knows no boundaries

Set some limits. How much of any category do you really need? How much is enough? Well, if you want to retain your sanity, what you keep is largely governed by the amount of storage space you have. If you don't want to be smothered by your stuff, you must set some limits. Remember: you have infinite capacity to bring things in but only finite capacity to store them. So let's talk about setting those limits. Setting limits is asking yourself what is a reasonable amount of any one item or category for you to have, given your family size, your lifestyle and your storage capacity. Once you set your limits, your limits will set you free.

There are three ways to set your limits: by number, by storage space or by date. Let's look at each in a bit more detail.

- *Limit by number*. Limiting by number is simply deciding on the number of items to keep in both primary and secondary storage. You may decide on 10 as a reasonable number of business shirts, or four as a reasonable number of frypans, or two bath towels per family member, plus an extra four for emergencies or guests. At the same time, limit the number you have in secondary storage. For example, 12 rolls of toilet paper, 10 cans of tomatoes or four bottles of shampoo. The choice is yours, but it will be made easier when you can actually see how many of these items you currently have. And — guess what — they are now sitting right in front of you in their sorted subcategories!

- *Limit by storage space*. Limiting by storage space means you limit by the amount of space you are prepared to dedicate to the items or category. One bookcase may be the storage space you decide on to store your books, or one drawer to store your socks, or one shelf of the pantry to store your canned food. You will have these items in front of you and will be able to see the space they currently take up. Are you willing to devote that much space to them in your allocated area?

- *Limit by date*. Limiting by date means using a date or a time frame when setting your limits. You may decide on keeping the latest 12 months of a car magazine, or the last 12 months of electricity accounts, or to keep tax deductible receipts for five years to comply with taxation requirements. It will be easy for you to set these date limits with the items sitting in front of you sorted into date order.

Whichever method you use, setting limits is a mindset and is essential for balancing your storage space and your stuff.

What's the bag limit?

Think back to the last time you flew to a holiday destination. Do you remember your flight? Do you remember the baggage limit you were set? Did you manage to have a great holiday with only 20 kilograms of baggage? Can you imagine how much you would have taken if there were no limits? The airline limit meant that you had to evaluate your baggage and only take the items that were necessary. Get the picture? Now you need to do this with your home. Only keep the items you use, need, want or love, and release the rest.

Hit the road, Jack!

Dispose of it! It's time for your clutter to leave the building or move to another room. The 'Bin it' items can be tossed into the rubbish and recycling bins. The 'Gift it' items can be given to family, friends or a charity. The 'Sell it' items can be stored somewhere until you have enough to warrant a garage or yard sale, or you can immediately put them up for sale online. The 'Move it' items get moved to their correct rooms or secondary storage areas, while items for repair go to the relevant repair area or person. It's important that everything leaves the scene of the crime as soon as humanly possible!

 ## Step 5: alloc8

Alloc8 is the third of the four action steps. In this step you allocate the most appropriate containers and the best possible locations for the things you use, need, want or love. Before reaching this step, you will have already decided what you are keeping in one or more categories.

Shopping time

You should now be able to see what you need to store and whether the existing storage is adequate or can be modified to suit. If the current storage is not adequate, now is the time to decide what you need to purchase to house it efficiently. It's important not to make these storage decisions until you reach this step. I've seen so many people go out and purchase containers, shelves and cupboards, and even hire external storage before they have reached this stage, only to find they haven't chosen the right type or amount for their needs. Please, please wait until this step to decide on storage adjustments and to make purchasing decisions. Now that you have decluttered your stuff, you'll most likely find you have sufficient space that requires just a few modifications. Before you go shopping for any new storage components, re-check all measurements. Remember the golden rule: measure twice, shop once!

Value your space

Not all space is the same. Like real estate, some areas are valued higher than others. Your space is no different. Generally, the areas that are easiest to get to, such as the fronts of shelves and areas within arm's reach of seated or standing positions, are considered to be primary storage areas. Backs of cupboards, high spaces and low spaces, under beds, and areas external to the house are considered to be secondary storage areas of the home. You need to know the difference and to convert as much secondary storage space to primary storage space as you can. Things you use infrequently and items surplus to your current needs belong in secondary storage space.

Your move

The key determinants to where you place items are based on how often you use them, their shape, size, weight and the overall category size. In addition, you need to take into account the room you have to work with and its configuration. The goal is to optimise your storage and make things as accessible as you can, in the least possible number of moves. My personal measure of success is that I can remove or replace anything in my home within two moves. You should aim to do the same.

In masterclass 4 you will learn all about storage options and how to make the most of your space. Right now, it's enough to know that after you have eliminated everything you no longer use, need, want or love, you will place what you are keeping into the most appropriate containers and storage.

 Step 6: activ8

Activ8 is the last of the four action steps. Roll up your sleeves because it's now time to get to work and reap the rewards of the consolidation, elimination and allocation steps. With the help of your tool kit, other members of the family or professionals, make any required adjustments to existing storage and install the new storage components you have purchased.

Spring clean

Give all storage areas a good spring clean. Some items will need to be dusted or cleaned before they are placed into their new clean storage locations.

Put it away

You can now go about putting all your stuff in its place. Like all the other action steps, the activ8 step can also be done in stages. It depends on the size of the room, the amount of stuff and the time you have available. Now is the time to label containers, shelves and drawers with their contents. Once everything is put away, finish off the spring clean by doing the floors, light fittings and windows.

 ## Step 7: evalu8

Evalu8 is the first of the two review steps. In this step you need to evaluate your system to see how it's working. Get your notebook out and go back to the notes you took during the 'Plan it' phase to make sure you have addressed all the issues you had with this room. Have you achieved your vision and your goals? Is the space physically, functionally and emotionally working for you? Are you easily able to locate, retrieve, use and replace every item you have deemed necessary to your lifestyle? Do you feel you have put your own personality into this room? Have you installed a system that has eliminated your frequent frustrations? Have you disposed of everything that needed to go? How do you feel now? In your notebook write a few notes on what you have achieved, how you did it and any improvements you can make in the next room to be organised.

Happy snaps

Now get your camera out and take your 'after' photos. Then compare them to your 'before' photos. What a difference! Can you believe it? It's done—and if you can do this room you can do the entire house. The in8steps system will be with you all the way.

Life is a journey

If you're happy with the result, leave it alone. If you've discovered anything that still isn't right, make some adjustments. Remember that things change! Babies are born, relationships change, children leave home and we change our jobs, our hobbies and our interests. Your stuff and your space will need to change in tandem with the changes in your life. The in8steps system can easily adapt to your evolving lifestyle, so continue to evaluate this room periodically and make the necessary changes.

 # Step 8: celebr8

Celebr8 is the second of the two review steps. In this step you should have the champagne on ice because you are almost done. You have achieved your vision and your goals. You have a room that is clean, organised and functional.

An ounce of prevention

> I hate housework! You make the beds, you do the dishes—and six months later you have to start all over again.
>
> **Joan Rivers**

Now is the time to take preventative measures to keep the room in check. There are tasks that must be done regularly. Create a home care schedule to manage regular home cleaning and maintenance. This will keep your home humming!

Timely tasks: specialise

There are various things that you do over and over again in every room of your home. In the laundry you have clothing to wash, dry and iron. In the bedrooms you have beds to make and sheets to change. In the bathrooms you have towels to change and supplies to top up. In the kitchen you have meals to make and dishes to wash, dry and put away. And in the office you have paperwork to complete. These actions are room specific.

Timely tasks: generalise

In addition to room-specific tasks, there are various regular general cleaning actions such as dusting, cleaning, vacuuming and floor washing to be done, usually on a weekly basis. Other regular maintenance actions such as cleaning windows, light fittings and soft furnishings are usually done monthly or quarterly. These actions are general and apply to all rooms.

Home care schedule

Set up your home care schedule in just three steps.

- List all the jobs that need to be done to keep your home clean, organised and functional.

- Add how often each job needs to be done — daily, weekly, monthly and so on.

- Create your home care schedule for cleaning and maintenance.

Your home care schedule will look something like this example in table 2.3 (overleaf).

Table 2.3: example of a home care schedule

Daily	Weekly	Monthly	Quarterly
Make beds	Change sheets	Wash doona covers	Rotate mattresses
Hang up clothes	Empty waste paper baskets	Vacuum soft furnishings	Wash mattress and pillow protectors
Wash, dry and iron clothes	Vacuum carpets and wash floors	Clean blinds	Clean windows
Empty kitchen bin	Dust furniture	Clean oven	Tidy pantry

Once you have created your home care schedule, be sure to do the following:

- *Lock it in.* Once you have listed the tasks and their frequency you just need to lock in times to do them. You can outsource jobs to other family members or to professionals, but the tasks need to be done by someone.

- *Raise the bar.* Now is the time to apply these time-saving techniques. Once you have organised your home you will set new standards, new rules and new rituals to keep your home clean, organised and functional.

- *Maintain it.* Your home care schedule is the backbone and lifeblood of your system. When you start from an organised base, you can forget about cleaning for hours and hours. Everything you do will take less time and energy than it used to.

Congratulations! It's time to celebrate. You did it!

Pop the cork!

It's time to collect your reward—and you have certainly earned it. On your journey you have created a well-organised home or room that you can be proud of. In the future you will enjoy the benefits of your work over and over again. You will be happy to share the results with your family and friends.

Putting it all together

Now you are familiar with all the steps in the in8steps system. You can see that while they follow a sequence, you can combine steps and fast-track whenever you like. You may be organising your children's wardrobe and right away you know you will need to raise the hanging rods and add a few extra shelves. Even though that is step 6, you are onto it already. You might already have an effective home care schedule that you use to clean the house, so you don't need to reinvent it. You will know what to do and how best to adapt the in8steps system to your own home, your lifestyle and your work preferences. Remember: it's just like driving a car—once you get the hang of it, it becomes automatic.

Now move on to masterclass 3: a space mission, where you will learn about the three elements of space.

Chapter 3

Masterclass 3: a space mission

A good home must be made, not bought.

Joyce Maynard

The three elements of space

Have you ever walked into a room and felt there was something wrong? You couldn't quite put your finger on it, but it didn't feel right. Chances are that one of the three elements of space was out of balance.

The three elements of space are:

- physical
- functional
- emotional.

When one or more element is out of balance, the room lacks something. That something can be fixed by finding which of the elements isn't working. By examining each of the elements you will be able to identify what's wrong with the room and correct it. Sometimes it's just a minor adjustment and at other times it requires a bit of rearranging of furniture and the introduction or removal of items to balance the space.

Let's get physical

All rooms have dimensions, layout, proportions, colour, lighting, aspects, views, temperature, storage capacity, furniture, accessories, fixtures and fittings, and a whole lot more. These are physical elements. If a room is too dark, or too hot, or has way too much in it for its size, or doesn't have enough storage, it needs to be reorganised.

Physical elements include:

- The size of the space and of the items within the space.

- The actual items in the space. Note style, age, shape, configuration, versatility and state of repair.

- The positioning within the space. Note locations of doors, power points, windows, heating ducts, return-air vents and cooling systems. Note the layout of the room and be aware of what is fixed and what is movable.

- The lighting in the space. Note the amount of natural and artificial lighting, window coverings and aspect of the room (whether it is facing north, south, east or west). Consider the natural lighting in different seasons as the lighting changes significantly season by season.

- The temperature, including heating and cooling of the space.

- The colours within the space.

- The capacity of the space. Note the quantities and type of stuff stored in the space and the amount of storage available.

Once you identify problematic physical elements, you can fix them. Sometimes it's the simple things — such as adding a few power points or a lamp, or moving a piece of furniture out of the room — that make a big difference.

Let's get functional

Every room has functions performed in it. Meals are cooked, TV is watched, people sleep, assignments are completed, books are read and written, laundry is washed, people bathe and cars are parked. If functions are performed with ease, the room can be called functional. If functions are difficult to perform, then the room is dysfunctional and needs to be reorganised or tweaked.

Functional elements include:

- The tasks that are performed in the space.

- The systems, processes, flows and routines undertaken in the space. Clutter zones are just bottlenecks in the system. They are evidence that there is a functional malfunction.

- The tools and equipment used to perform the functions of life and the instructions that assist with the functions. An oven and a computer are physical elements in a room, but if you don't have the instructions to make them work, they are not functional.

- The names used to describe the space. The names we give to rooms and spaces sometimes dictate how we treat them. Names, such as kitchen, bedroom, junk room, spare room, junk drawer, landing and storage shed, all elicit meanings and attract items. What do you put in your junk drawer or on the landing?

- The labels attached to items and files. Labels declare to everyone an intention to keep things in order. They are used on containers to let people know about their contents and save time and energy by quickly and easily leading us to what we want.

- The access to the space. Is it too high, too low, at eye level, at waist level or is it an awkward corner?

- The users of the space. Who uses the space and how is it used? Kitchens, for example, have many users, and adults and children see the space very differently. Safety and access are very important. Children need to be able to reach items they need, but not the poisons or medications. Adults like to have everyday items within arm's reach. The aged or disabled may need extra devices to improve a room's functionality.

> ## Tip
>
> A good test of functionality is to check whether you can remove, use and replace an item within one or two movements. If you can't, it's time for some reorganisation.

Let's get emotional

Rooms elicit feelings too! Go to the doorway of any room in your home and ask yourself how this room makes you feel. Some answers I have heard include happy, calm, confused, depressed, overwhelmed and sad. Emotions can be lifted by adding items such as photos, artwork, flowers, music, candles, soft furnishings, colour and sentimental items to a room.

Your rooms should express your personality and give you positive emotional responses.

Emotional elements include all of the feelings evoked by the space, including:

- warm or cool feelings
- welcoming or unwelcoming feelings
- calm or chaotic feelings
- personal feelings such as confidence, control, empowerment, authenticity, comfort and freedom.

Use your knowledge of the three elements of space to bring every room in your home back into harmony. Refer to this masterclass whenever you feel one of your rooms doesn't feel right and pinpoint the problem.

Mission accomplished! Now move on to masterclass 4: getting a handle on hardware, where I will reveal my five secret weapons for organising your home.

Chapter 4

Masterclass 4: getting a handle on hardware

A friend is the only person you will let into the house when you are 'turning out drawers'.

Pam Brown

Some storage secrets

Most people embark on their organising journey without a clue about storage hardware. You won't be making this mistake. Instead, you'll arm yourself with some insider secrets, so you'll know exactly what will and what won't work in any storage situation. You'll learn about the little idiosyncrasies of shelves, drawers, hanging rods, hooks and containers. By understanding the components that make up a space, you'll make informed choices about what to do, instead of running off to the shops and coming back with storage hardware you don't need.

> **Please wait!**
>
> One of the keys to organising is that you organise first and shop last. You can make do with what you have until you know what you really need. You don't know what you really need until you have sorted through your stuff. So remember, shopping happens last.

Arm yourself

Did you know that your storage hardware arsenal is made up of only five basic components? So it makes sense to understand how they work, what they can do and how to put them together to form the best possible storage solutions in your home. They are your secret weapons!

Secret weapon 1: shelves

A shelf is a shelf, is a shelf, is a shelf...No it isn't! Shelves have great strengths but they also have limitations. By understanding how they work, you can implement solutions to overcome any weaknesses in your existing or future shelving.

Delving into shelving

Shelves are mostly made from melamine, timber, glass, plastic or wire. Choose a material to suit your storage needs and situation. Use waterproof shelving in wet areas, timber or glass in living rooms, or cabinets and melamine in the pantry.

Width, depth and thickness

The width, depth and thickness of a shelf can affect its strength:

- The wider the shelf, the weaker it becomes, so limit the weight it carries.

- If overloaded, a shelf may bow in the middle and eventually collapse.

- Distribute weight along a shelf, keeping heavier items towards the supported ends.

- You can reinforce a shelf with extra shelf pins or batons to strengthen it.

- Glue two shelves together to provide additional strength.

- To stop the shelves bowing, try turning them over occasionally if they're reversible.

The size of a shelf can affect how practical it is to store items:

- If shelves are to be used to store folded clothing or linen, aim for widths in multiples of 300 mm.

- Shelves of 300 mm, 600 mm, 900 mm and 1200 mm widths enable neat stacks of folded items to be stored with no wastage of space.

- A 500 mm shelf is too wide for most folded items and isn't wide enough for two stacks side by side.

The 'same: same' technique

Deep shelves always seem to hide stuff at the back, making access difficult. You have to remove everything to find the item you need. But there is a solution to this problem and I like to call it the 'same: same' technique. You simply use two identical containers, each half the size of the depth of the shelf, and place one in the front and one in the back. In order to get to the back storage area, you only have to remove one item—the front container. You can use this technique with most types of containers, boxes or magazine boxes. Place items you use less frequently in the rear position. Then label the shelf or the front container to indicate what's stored in front and what's stored behind. Of course, label the rear container as well.

Alternatively, you can stick a cupboard storage guide on the inside of the cupboard door to indicate where items are stored. See this technique in figure 4.1.

Figure 4.1: 'same: same' in action

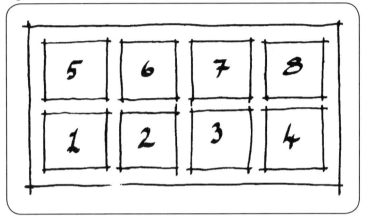

The 'same: same' technique works well in many situations:

- Have folded bath towels in the front and back layer of a shelf.

- Have household bath towels in the front and guest towels or beach towels in the back.

- For seasonal clothing, for example, put winter clothing behind and summer clothing in front.

- In a pantry you could have older stock in the front and fresher reserve stock behind it.

- With files, put last year's folders in the back, with the current year's folders in the front.

The 'many: few' technique

The back of deep shelves can also be used effectively by placing a row of items vertically at the back, followed by a few boxes of items at the front. I like to call it the 'many: few' technique: 'many' in the back with 'few' in the front. In order to get to the back storage area, you only have to remove one or two items in the front. Place items you use less frequently in the rear position. Then label the shelf or the front containers to indicate what's stored in front and what's stored behind. Alternatively, you can stick a cupboard storage guide on the inside of the cupboard door showing where items are stored. See the 'many: few' technique in figure 4.2.

Figure 4.2: 'many: few' in action

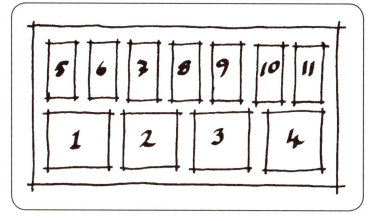

The 'many: few' technique works well in many situations:

- Have sets of party glasses (the many) at the back of a deep cupboard, with a couple of containers in the front (the few).

- In your laundry cupboard, have a row of vases at the back of a deep cupboard, with a few stacks of towels in front of them.

- In a children's room, place a row of books at the rear of a deep cupboard, with a few boxes of toys in front of them.

- In a deep bookcase, place a row of novels at the back and a few stacks of books in front. Remove one stack to reveal the titles of the novels.

Fixed and adjustable shelves

Fixed shelves are set in place and cannot be moved. Adjustable shelves can easily be moved, removed or added. The position of adjustable shelves depends on the drilled holes available. You can always drill extra holes to make them even more versatile or to add an extra shelf between your fixed shelves. The number of shelves you need in a cupboard or unit depends on what you're storing, but as a general rule plan for more shelves rather than fewer. Most cupboards can use at least one extra shelf.

Reach the heights

When organising shelving that's above eye level, it's always best to store tall, light items on the top shelf. This makes the items on this shelf easier to reach, enabling you to access them without needing a stepladder. For instance, the top shelf of a pantry could have two or three tall containers holding spare cereal, crackers, napkins, packs of sauces or soups, paper plates or any other lightweight items. In another cupboard, the top shelf could have a container with the attachments for your appliances while another tall container may hold baking tinware such as trays, cake tins and muffin pans all standing up on their sides.

The low down

For shelving units that go down to floor level, store tall and heavy items on the lowest shelf. Place them into containers that are easy to slide out. If the floor is the bottom shelf, as in a walk-in pantry or wardrobe, use containers on castors on the floor (under the lowest shelf) so they can be rolled out when needed or for cleaning.

Close the gap

To best utilise your shelving, you want as little unused space as possible between the shelves. This is why adjustable shelves are ideal. Store items of roughly the same height on a shelf, as a combination of tall and low items creates pockets of unused space. You can create uniformity by using a row of identical-height containers and work to that height.

Behind closed doors

If you have a set of shelves behind cupboard doors, consider using the back of the doors as storage to hang things from. To do this you have to be sure the hung items fit when the doors are closed. If you need a bit more room, remove the shelves and cut a bit off the back to create the gap you need at the front. This is ideal for spice racks on the doors of pantries or jewellery holders on the backs of wardrobe doors.

Irregular shelves

Irregular shelves are not standard in shape or style. They may be corner shelves, cut-away shelves in pantries or custom-made shelves in tricky spaces.

Stepping up

Step shelves are shelves with side supports and are used to create extra layers of storage in certain situations—such as in corner cupboards or when the space is really wide and a regular shelf can't be installed easily. Step shelves are great because they are portable, so you can move them around whenever you like. They are very easy to make and can be made to any size to suit your needs.

Cornered

Corner cupboards have deep recesses that are very difficult to access. Due to their shape, shelves in corner cupboards generally need to be fitted at the time of construction and are difficult, if not impossible, to install or remove afterwards.

A clever way to deal with corner cupboards is to use a number of identical containers of a depth and height slightly smaller than the depth and height of the shelves in the corner cupboard. Place the containers along one back wall of the cupboard so that the container closest to the door opening slides out easily and freely. Then place another container or two against the other back wall, with at least one of them able to slide forward freely through the other door opening. That way, to access anything in the cupboard you only need to move a container or two. Store infrequently used items, such as Christmas tableware or picnic items, in deep corners, and plastic containers, plastic tableware or baking pans in the containers closest to the door. There are also purpose-built solutions available — such as lazy Susans — to solve your corner cupboard problems. Corner cupboards can work brilliantly for pots and pans. Place pots and pans, complete with lids, onto shelves with handles facing forward. Add a shallow shelf at the top to accommodate your frypans. See how you can negotiate corners in figure 4.3.

Figure 4.3: corners in action

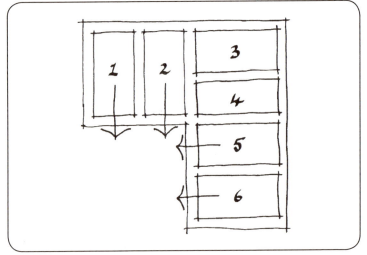

Roll on

Roll-out shelves are really just drawers. However, as they are called 'roll-out shelves' they are mentioned here. These are shelves that roll out on runners—like drawers—but are hidden behind cupboard doors. They often replace shelves in under-bench storage, particularly in kitchens. They are ideal for storing crockery, everyday glassware, salad bowls, bakeware, and pots and pans.

Secret weapon 2: drawers

Drawers are by far everyone's favourite storage component because they hide a multitude of sins and create the illusion that everything is neat and tidy.

Win, lose or drawer?

Where would we be without drawers? By simply pulling on a handle you can make their contents come out to greet you. With a gentle push it all goes away, out of sight and out of mind.

Drawers, like shelves, can be made from a variety of materials, mainly melamine, timber, plastic and wire. Choose a material to suit your storage needs and situation. Drawers have width, depth, height and varying base strength.

Drawn and quartered

Drawers work perfectly for storage at chest height and lower. You need to be able to peer into the drawer in order to use it effectively. Shelves work best at eye level and above.

Utilise the height of drawers. This is the measurement of the clearance space between the internal base of a drawer and the bottom of the front face of the drawer above it. For top drawers, measure from the internal base of the drawer to the bottom of the fixing rail. Use these measurements to determine the maximum container height you can use in each drawer.

Measure all drawers separately, even if they look the same. The top drawer will almost always have a different height measurement than the rest of a set of drawers with identical front faces.

Divide and conquer

Drawers benefit hugely by having compartments, dividers or partitions. These create sections for contents that are prone to move about when the drawers are opened and closed. If you have some spare timber in the garage it's easy to make your own drawer dividers and you can make them to the exact specifications you need. Where would we be without our cutlery drawer dividers?

Tip

By strategically placing a few dividers into a drawer you can create several compartments.

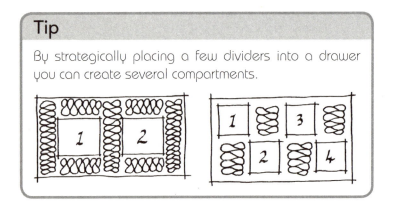

Dead end

For drawers that don't fully extend, be careful not to create dead space at the back. It's easy to have things trapped at

the back. Dead space usually measures between 0 and 50 mm depending on the size of the drawer and the runners used. Always use a divider that allows access to the back of the drawer.

Droopy drawers

Overfilling drawers can cause bases to sag and drawers to stick, especially if you push the contents down while closing the drawer. You unintentionally place extra pressure on both the base and the runners.

Quick on the drawer

Drawers move in and out on runners. These runners can be fully extended or partially extended. A fully extended runner allows the drawer to roll out completely while a partially extended runner leaves a small section of the back of the drawer less accessible. It's important to know this when configuring your drawers.

Check runner strength and don't overload drawers beyond their weight capacity. Aim for fully extendable runners where possible, affordable and practical.

Double drawers have two layers of drawers within a single drawer and are particularly useful for storage of cutlery, utensils and even jewellery.

Kickboard drawers are drawers built into the kickboards of kitchens to utilise this otherwise wasted space. You can use these shallow drawers for bakeware, roasting pans, trays and platters.

Secret weapon 3: hanging rods

Whenever I go into clothing shops I just love the way everything hangs freely on hanging rods. All the hangers are the same and there is space between items. It's a pleasure to run your hand over every item on the rack. Above all, items are easy to remove and replace.

Just hangin' around

Hanging rods come in a range of materials: chrome, wood, plastic and aluminium are the most common. Choose a material to suit your storage needs and situation.

While mostly found in wardrobes to hang dresses, shirts, skirts and trousers, hanging rods are sometimes installed in laundries to hang clothing waiting to dry, to be ironed or to be put away.

Hanging rods have length, shape and strength. Stronger, rectangular hanging rods are slowly replacing their popular, but weaker, round friends.

Aim for a length that will hold the weight of its load without sagging. You can use extra supports along the way to assist. The longer the hanging rod, the more supports you need.

Hanging rods can be attached to the side walls or to the underside of a shelf. When attached to the underside of adjustable shelves, it's really easy to move your hanging rods up and down in line with the latest hem lengths or the ages of your children. Many wardrobes are now fitted with easy-to-move hanging-rod supports, making adjustments easier. There are also easy-to-attach trapeze-like devices that allow you to hang a new rod off an existing one, giving you twice the hanging space.

Get the height right

Aim to have a range of heights for your hanging rods to suit the range of lengths of your clothing. Create sections for long, medium and short clothing. For example, you might need to accommodate long gowns, dresses, shirts, skirts and trousers. Work out your needs and fix your hanging rods accordingly. Optimise your hanging space in three simple steps.

- For each section, hang the longest item belonging to that section onto your hanging rod, complete with coathanger.

- Then move the rod up and down until you have a 50 mm to 100 mm clearance between the floor and the bottom of your garment.

- Finally, mark that spot and attach your hanging rod.

Having all your clothing hanging 50 mm to 100 mm above the floor gives you these great benefits:

- It discourages you from putting things on the floor as there is little room.

- You can vacuum and clean the floor with ease by just skimming under the clothing.

- With your hanging rods set at the lowest height for each situation you gain extra storage on the shelves above.

When using double layers of hanging rods, adjust the bottom hanging rod first and then set the higher hanging rod to the longest item, ensuring it clears the rod below by 50 mm to 100 mm.

Odd rods

Over-the-door hanging rods are convenient for hanging clothing that needs drying, airing, ironing or sorting. Hydraulic pull-down hanging rods are great for rooms with high ceilings as they allow you to hang clothing in high and often wasted space. Just use the pull-down lever to bring the rod down when required.

Secret weapon 4: hooks

Anyone who has a key hook knows how handy hooks can be. Whenever a hook is hung it's usually for a specific need, such as for hanging the dog's lead near the back door or for hanging the children's school bags on before and after school. Often it's the first thing that comes to mind for a quick fix for solving many of life's frequent frustrations! When I first became a mother, I installed a few removable hooks on the back of the bedroom doors to hold towels for my children. So handy! The towels don't clutter up the rest of the room, the children can reach them easily and I could easily adjust the hooks and remove them when they were no longer needed. A simple but effective 'hook' solution.

Hooks are a quick and easy way to add extra storage almost anywhere. Whether on walls, behind doors or on the sides of bookcases, a few well-placed hooks can work wonders.

Hooks include fixed or removable hooks, over-the-door hooks, hanging hooks, and fixed and free-standing coat racks.

If hooks take your fancy, here are some tips for using them:

- Ensure hooks can hold the weight of the items hanging from them. You don't want a hook and its contents falling in the middle of the night!

- S-shaped hooks can be hung from hanging rods and eliminate the need to have hooks on walls.

- Consider using a noticeboard or magnetic board with a range of hooks on it if you have a number of items to hang.

- Use hooks to hang bags, scarves and belts in wardrobes, extension cords in laundries, coats and hats in entrances, calendars on walls or kitchen doors, or jewellery on the backs of wardrobe doors.

Secret weapon 5: containers

Containers are the most popular storage solution. Just look in your plastics cupboard to see how far your obsession for containers has progressed. Many people purchase containers just for the look of them, without knowing what they will be used for. Most of these containers remain empty, cluttering up cupboards and waiting patiently to be of use. Containers love nothing more than being put to work, safeguarding the items that fill them. They happily live in drawers minding your paperclips, sit on shelves storing your sugar and hang from rods protecting your evening gown. They require minimal maintenance, they never take a holiday and they only complain when they are overstuffed!

Containers are used to hold, store or transport one or more items. They keep items clean and fresh and come in all shapes and sizes. The range includes boxes, plastic tubs, cutlery trays, jars, tins, cans and bins. The key to container use is to choose a container that is compatible with both the items stored and the storage location.

Break down the bulk

It's always better to use more containers of a smaller size than fewer containers of a larger size. The larger the container, the more it holds, the heavier it gets and the harder it is to store. If you break a large container down to two to three smaller containers you reduce the weight and the bulk and increase the storage options. The smaller containers are easier to lift, move, stack and store. Reserve the use of large containers for light items.

Load 'em up

When filling your containers with sets of rigid items—such as CDs and DVDs in your living spaces or packets of soup in your pantry—follow these five steps.

■ Load contents as vertically as possible for easy visibility and access. When filling a container, it's sometimes easier to load the container while it's standing on its side.

■ Place items across the shortest distance between sides, rather than along the longest distance where they will have more space to fall.

■ Aim to fill any container to only 90 per cent of its capacity to allow for easy access, removal and replacement of contents.

■ If the container is less than 90 per cent full, use a filler—such as scrunched-up paper—to fill the gap until you have more items to store. This stops the contents falling about and stabilises the container.

■ Use dividers to break containers into sections if necessary.

Creating contented containers

Keep the following in mind and you'll find that containers are an indispensible storage item.

■ If containers stack easily, they require less storage space when not in use.

■ Having clear containers and lids lets you see their contents from any angle.

■ Lids are optional in many circumstances, so use open containers when you can.

■ Unless you are intentionally colour coding, use neutral or transparent containers.

- Aim for uniformity to create a clean look and so that you can mix and match.

- Keep in mind that round containers take up more space and are harder to arrange.

- Choose containers with castors for floor storage.

- Label your containers so you know what's in them.

Now that you have a handle on your hardware, it's time to learn some time-saving techniques that will turn your organising work into organising play! So read on.

in8 time-saving techniques

in8minutes	Beat the clock and power up.
in8stretch	Draw it out and take each task one step further.
in8links	Tie tasks to days of the week, times of the day or other activities.
in8limits	Limit your stuff and your limits will set you free.
in8rules	Lay down the law and live by your rules.
in8focus	Put up the barriers and stay on track.
in8names	Name it and claim it.
in8rituals	Make it routine and form new habits.

Chapter 5

Masterclass 5: time-saving techniques

Work expands so as to fill the time available for its completion.

C. Northcote Parkinson

It's the little things

Sometimes little things have a big impact. The following in8time-saving techniques are little things you can do when you get bitten by the procrastination bug! We all try to put things off at times even though we know it will take us twice as long to do it later on! Later is the best friend of clutter and everything we put off is just more unfinished business cluttering up our homes and our heads.

Learn the following in8time-saving techniques and use them whenever you feel the need for that turbo boost of power!

Beat the clock: in8minutes

You know how quickly you can do something when you are under pressure. Remember the last time someone gave you short notice that they were coming to visit? You did a quick run around and achieved amazing things in a very short time. The house looked great and you enjoyed the occasion knowing all the clutter was safely parked in the laundry. With in8minutes you create the same sense of urgency by using a timer to speed up your performance. Try this: set a timer for eight minutes. Go to your bathroom and put things away, change the towels and do a general tidy up. I bet it takes *less than* eight minutes to do! It's not a spring clean but the bathroom looks very presentable. Pump yourself up with in8minute power bursts to do those mundane jobs around the house or small sections of your reorganising project. I have two favourite in8minute power bursts.

- *The in8minute email purge.* I set the timer, write down how many emails I have in my inbox and then power away. Ding, ding, ding and eight minutes later I can see just how many emails I have deleted, replied to or moved to folders. Once I see just how much can be done in8minutes, I often set the timer to go another round and after a few sessions my inbox is clear again. Such a relief!

- *The in8minute room run-around.* I set the timer for eight minutes per room in my house. I race around doing a quick straighten up and tidy, and the house is instantly fit for visitors or for the cleaners to do their thing!

Draw it out: in8stretch

This technique involves taking a task one little step further than usual. If you normally make breakfast and leave everything out while you sit down to eat, why not stretch the task to include putting away whatever you can *before* you sit down to eat? Here are two of my favourite in8stretches.

- I fold items as soon as I remove them from the clothes line or dryer, which saves on ironing time.

- I cook extra portions of casserole or soup for freezing, which saves on cooking time later on.

What in8stretches can you put into your daily routine?

Tie them up: in8links

Have you ever gone through a week, or even a month, and realised you haven't changed the sheets or watered the plants? If you leave tasks to when you think about them, they often get neglected. in8links is a simple technique that links routine tasks to other routine tasks or memorable dates or times. If you regularly change the bed linen and do the washing on Saturday or do the ironing while watching your favourite TV show, you are already using in8links without realising it. Why not link watering the plants to rubbish collection day or washing the car to the last Sunday of the month or to when the lawns are cut? Link tasks to days of the week, times of the day or other activities such as your favourite TV show. How many tasks can you link up?

Put a lid on it: in8limits

How much is enough? The biggest issue with clutter in a disorganised home is the sheer quantity! Everyone is packed to the rafters with stuff. We are all suffering from *stuffocation*, which is a symptom of *affluenza*! A simple way to reduce what you have is to apply in8limits to every category and make a decision on how much is enough for your current lifestyle. How many pairs of shoes, handbags, shirts, trousers, wine glasses, towels, books, DVDs, TVs and radios are enough? I have placed limits on just about everything in my home and office. For example:

- *Towels.* I have three per person in our home and two spares for guests. I now have loads of extra space in my linen cupboard.

- *Sheets.* I have two sets per bed, one on the bed and one in the wash or in the linen cupboard. This means no more stuffy, stale sheets.

It is a revelation to discover just how much you really have and liberating when you make a conscious decision on how much is enough. Your limits will set you free!

Lay down the law: in8rules

I really admire people who can say they *always* do something or they *never* do something else. For example: 'I never leave the toilet seat up', 'I always wash my hands before cooking', 'I never go to bed until the kitchen is tidy and everything is put away' or 'I never go shopping without a shopping list'. in8rules work really well for resolving your frequent frustrations and irritations. Once you identify the frustrations, create a new rule to eliminate them from your life. If you are always searching for misplaced reading glasses, allocate one spot to place them and make the rule, 'I always place my reading glasses in the bowl in the kitchen'. Most rules include *always* or *never* because that is what makes the difference between a rule and a wish. If you say, 'I will try to make my bed every morning', it's not a rule, it's just a wish! What rules can you set for yourself to overcome your frequent frustrations? What rules do you already use? Are your current rules moving you forward or holding you back?

Put up the barriers: in8focus

Do you start things and then get distracted along the way? If you do, then try some in8 focus techniques to make you more efficient and focused on the task at hand. If you have some important paperwork to do, try locking yourself in the study. This stops others interrupting you and stops you from escaping from the room! You can write your tasks on a piece of paper and stick it on the wall to remind you of what you are doing. Have a special uniform to wear while undertaking certain activities. You could wear a tracksuit for house cleaning or an apron for cooking. I have tried all these measures and they work. I regularly tie myself to my office chair until I finish what I set out to do! I always wear an apron when cooking, and my training gear when cleaning or decluttering. Make it fun, experiment and see what works for you.

Give it an alias: in8names

This technique changes your perceptions by renaming and reclaiming your space. If you call a drawer a junk drawer, guess what? Junk will live in that drawer! If you call a room a spare room, all of the spare stuff will gather there. So why not elevate the space by assigning a new and meaningful name to it? Names such as guest room, study, tea-towel drawer, library, sewing room and linen cupboard describe the space and what goes into it. I used to call the top of our stairs the landing and lots of stuff ended up landing there. I now call the space the library and have installed shelving along the walls to store all my books. The whole area has taken on a new personality and nothing just lands there anymore. For a short time it may help to use labels to remind you of what goes where, but once you get used to calling a space by its new name, the space will conform to its name. Naming also means labelling. Where necessary or appropriate, use labels to remind you of what goes where.

Make it routine: in8rituals

These are a series of activities performed in a sequence. You can set up a morning and an evening ritual, a mealtime ritual or a study ritual. It involves looking at all the activities and steps you need to undertake, estimating the time they will take and thereby creating a sort of procedure. Here is an example of a morning ritual:

- Get up and make the bed as it would be made in a five-star hotel.

- Get dressed for exercise.

- Have a cup of hot water and lemon juice and then exercise.

- Have breakfast, shower and get dressed for the day.

- Take any washing to the laundry and remove anything that does not belong in the bedroom or bathroom.

Once you get used to using a few rituals, these become habits that comfort and support you along the way. You go into autopilot mode and everything is so much easier to do.

Use the in8time-saving techniques and use them often. Mix them up, combine them and then see what happens. Any time you get stuck, pick a technique to help get you unstuck. As you will see in the next two chapters, these techniques can be applied to any room of your home and will make getting organised much more fun.

Chapter 6

Bedroom boost

Women usually love what they buy, yet hate two-thirds of what is in their closets.

Mignon McLauchlin

Bedroom boost and wardrobe workout

There is nothing more soothing than walking into your bedroom to find the bed made as in a five-star hotel, the room looking clean and tidy, a framed photo of the family by the bedside lamp and an organised wardrobe full of clothes you love to wear. If you think this is just a dream, you are not alone. The reality is that horizontal wardrobes, better known as 'floordrobes', are rapidly replacing vertical ones! Clothing is draped over furniture, strewn across floors and piled into corners. Bedrooms across the country are littered with old reading material, dirty tissues and half-empty coffee cups. It's time to wake up from this nightmare!

Your bedroom is the first thing you see every morning and the last thing you see every night. It's the one room in the home where you can really express your personality and that you can call your own. Bedrooms are fun to organise because you get reacquainted with your wardrobe, discovering long-forgotten treasures and quite a few fashion disasters along the way. Together we'll create a bedroom that is clean, organised and functional!

Now read on and I'll reveal the in8steps system checklist that you can use for any room in your house.

in8steps at a glance

Tick the boxes as you complete the steps.

 ## Step 1: initi8 the process

☐ Identify your frequent frustrations.

☐ Set your vision and your goals.

☐ Gather your tools: set up your organising, cleaning and tool kits.

☐ Get in the mood: dress for success, turn up the music and have refreshments on hand.

 ## Step 2: investig8 what you have

☐ Note the physical, functional and emotional elements.

☐ Draw a floor plan and take measurements as required.

☐ Discover what's in your cupboards, on shelves and in drawers. Get an overview.

☐ Note anything you need to purchase or fix.

☐ Take 'before' photos.

 **Step 3: consolid8 into big fat categories**

☐ Set up 'Bin it', 'Gift it', 'Sell it' and 'Move it' containers.

☐ Determine your big fat categories and subcategories.

☐ Sort everything into big fat categories and subcategories.

Step 4: elimin8 what you don't use, need, want or love

☐ When in doubt about an item, ask it the critical elimination questions:

- Do I use you? If so, how often? When was the last time? When will be the next time?

- Do I need you? Could I borrow you or substitute you with something else?

- Do I really want you or just the memory of you or where you came from? To preserve the memory, take a photo!

- Do I love you? Are you of sufficient sentimental value for me to keep?

☐ Set limits for both primary and secondary storage using number, space and date as a guide.

☐ Release it! Bin the trash, gift items to charity or friends, sell items of value and move things back to their correct rooms or to secondary storage.

Step 5: alloc8 containers and locations for what you are keeping

☐ Purchase any new storage components you need. Recheck measurements first.

☐ Allocate storage space and make any necessary adjustments.

 ## Step 6: activ8 your space

☐ Thoroughly clean the room, including all storage surfaces and interiors.

☐ Adjust or install storage components as necessary.

☐ Place items into their new containers and locations.

☐ Label containers, shelves and drawers as appropriate.

 ## Step 7: evalu8 how it's working

☐ Have your frequent frustrations been addressed?

☐ Have you achieved your vision and your goals for this space?

☐ Does the room physically, functionally and emotionally please you?

☐ Make adjustments and finetune the system until it's running smoothly.

☐ Take 'after' photos.

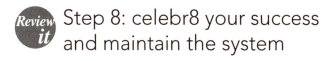

Step 8: celebr8 your success and maintain the system

- ☐ Create a list of tasks needed for regular cleaning and maintenance.

- ☐ Lock your tasks into your home care schedule.

- ☐ Raise the bar and set new standards, new rules and rituals.

- ☐ Congratulations! It's time to celebrate. You did it!

- ☐ Collect your reward. You certainly deserve it!

Before you begin

Before you start organising your bedroom, make the bed and place a clean sheet on top to give you a clear sorting surface to work on. Take any dirty clothing to the laundry and bring any clean clothing belonging to that bedroom back with you. Better still, bring the washing and ironing totally up to date prior to organising your bedrooms. If you have a portable clothes rack or an over-the-door laundry holder, now is the time to get them out. Have an additional box in which to store old wire coathangers which, hopefully, after your wardrobe workout, will be replaced by a new set of good quality coathangers. Once that's done, grab your notebook and let's get started!

Step 1: initi8

Note your frequent frustrations. Are your clothes squashed together in drawers or on shelves, requiring them to be ironed for a second time? Do you find it impossible to vacuum your walk-in wardrobe because of all the shoes and clutter on the floor? Do you often face the dilemma of trying to decide which clothes are clean and which are dirty among the piles in the bedroom corner? Maybe it's the time you waste searching through crowded racks of clothes but finding nothing you want to wear that frustrates you. Do you resent that extra 15 minutes wasted every morning, frantically racing around getting ready for work, knowing that it sets the tone for the rest of the day?

Set your vision and your goals, gather your tools and get in the mood.

 **Step 2: investig8**

Physically, bedrooms contain both built-in and free-standing furniture such as beds, side tables, chests of drawers, wardrobes, chairs, lamps, TVs, clocks and decorator items. They may also contain desks, gym equipment and toys. Bedrooms come in all shapes and sizes and furniture can be configured in a variety of ways. Bedrooms vary in the number of occupants, and they need to satisfy the requirements of each of them. Most of what is stored in bedrooms amounts to wardrobe items.

Functionally, bedrooms primarily provide for sleep. But many other functions are performed in this room, such as resting, dressing and undressing, reading, studying, romancing, playing, escaping and convalescing.

Emotionally, the bedroom has the most potential for personal expression. This room offers a lot of freedom in terms of decorating and organising to suit personal taste. A cluttered bedroom can emotionally cripple an occupant, but a bedroom can also be a real haven, a sanctuary and a very restful place if organised appropriately.

But pretty much, bedrooms are just one big wardrobe with a bed! So if we fix our wardrobes, the bedroom is finally free to fulfil its potential.

Step 3: consolid8

Sort your bedroom items into big fat categories. Lay out your sorting containers and group items together, throwing out as much as possible along the way. Here is a list of typical bedroom big fat categories with their subcategories. Use them or create your own:

- *underwear:* underpants, panties, girdles, bras, vests, singlets, spencers, camisoles, petticoats, slips, pantyhose and socks

- *sleepwear:* pyjamas, nightdresses, robes and dressing gowns

- *outerwear:* coats, jackets, raincoats, skirts, trousers, jeans, shorts, shirts, blouses, t-shirts, tops, vests, jumpers, sweaters, cardigans, dresses and evening wear

- *footwear:* shoes, boots, sandals, slippers, runners, trainers, sand shoes, sports shoes, thongs and flip-flops

- *accessories:* handbags, briefcases, satchels, scarves, belts, watches, jewellery, ties, hats, handkerchiefs and gloves

- *sportswear:* casual, leisure, track pants, sweat tops, gym, swimwear, and specialist sports or team wear (such as ski or tennis gear)

- *travel items:* suitcases, overnight bags, toiletry bags and travel accessories (such as adapters, neck pillows and shoe bags)

- *linen items:* bed linen, blankets, comforters, bed spreads, pillows, under-blankets and mattress protectors (and maybe towels, face washers, bath mats and robes)

- *children's toys:* dolls, prams, dolls' houses, games, trucks and more

- *reading material:* books, magazines and catalogues.

Layer it!

As well as organising your items by type you may like to add a few extra layers to make your wardrobe really rock! You will already be doing this instinctively, but it still pays to have a look at your options before you begin the consolidation process. Additional layers can include by person, season, size or function.

Multi-layer it!

Feel free to combine as many layers as you like. For example, if you wear a uniform to work, you might like to bring all uniform items together. Have a drawer, shelf and hanging section just for uniform items, making it easy to dress in the morning, instead of rummaging around all over the place. This works particularly well for children's school uniforms. Perhaps you should separate your T-shirts into a number of locations. You may put a few on a shelf together with your gym wear, a couple together with your gardening or painting clothes and perhaps one to keep with your swimwear. Once you get the hang of it you will have lots of fun discovering what works best for you.

 # Step 4: elimin8

Eliminate as much as you can by asking the following critical questions of each item you are unsure about:

- Do I wear you? If so, how often? When was the last time? When will be the next time?

- Do I need you? Do you go with other items in my wardrobe?

- Do I really want you? Do you suit and flatter my current body shape?

- Do I love you? Do I receive compliments when I wear you?

Create a working wardrobe

Fashions change, your body shape changes, your job changes and your lifestyle changes, so why are the same old clothes hanging around in your wardrobe? Think about who you are, what you do and how you want to present yourself to the world. By releasing your unflattering or hardly worn garments, you can create a wardrobe that works: one that's easy to dress from and that makes you feel and look good, regardless of where you need to go or what you need to do. The things you release will have a new life elsewhere and you will have a new lease of life as well!

Partner up

While you are deciding on what stays and what goes, you will discover items you love, but have never worn. It could be that you still love them and want to wear them but you don't have other pieces to go with them. For example, you may have a great skirt but no top to wear with it. We refer to that skirt as being unattached and your job is to find a partner for it. So take it shopping to find a top or jacket to turn it into a perfect match!

Your limits will set you free

Set limits on what will be stored in primary and secondary bedroom storage space and how much you want in secondary storage space elsewhere. How many t-shirts, skirts, black trousers, jackets, scarves, handbags, shoes or underpants are enough? Consider the amount of storage you have and the users of the room.

Step 5: alloc8

Allocate containers and locations for what you are keeping. The advantage now is that you can see exactly how much stuff and space you have. The trick is to match the stuff with the space. If you still have clothing in the laundry awaiting washing or ironing, be sure to allow space for it when it returns to the wardrobe. Better still, bring the washing and ironing totally up to date prior to organising your bedroom.

Organise your bedroom by allocating space by person, by function (such as work clothing or sports clothing), or by type or shape of item (such as scarves, long tops, short tops, dresses or trousers). The choice is yours, and you can combine them. Do whatever makes sense to you.

Storage smarts for bedrooms

Refer to masterclass 4: getting a handle on hardware for a quick refresher, if necessary. When organising the bedroom consider the amount of storage space you have and your priorities.

Following are some guidelines for bedroom storage.

An undercover affair

Organise your underwear:

- When you find a pair of undies you love, buy as many pairs as you need in a typical week and then add a couple of spares. As they start to wear out, find another pair you love and repeat the process. Do the same with bras, camisoles, singlets and so on. Remember your shape, your needs and your taste will change, so don't purchase too much of anything.

- Keep 'special occasion' undies separate from your day-to-day wear. Zip-lock bags work really well for these.

- Place rolled-up pantyhose or tights of the same type and colour in zip-lock bags or containers. Dressing will be a dream without the annoyance of rummaging through tangled tights and hosiery.

- Dispose of hosiery with ladders or holes immediately. Or place slightly imperfect hosiery in a separate zip-lock bag for wearing under trousers for extra warmth in winter.

- Keep socks in their pairs, rolled up or folded over and keep like colours grouped together.

- Place socks into containers in drawers. Shoeboxes are a great divider to start with.

Pyjama party

Organise your sleepwear:

- Hang dressing gowns and robes on hooks in the bathroom or bedroom. This item is likely to be the longest garment in your wardrobe, but it's silly to have a hanging rod set at a height for just one or two garments. It's better to fold robes not in use and hang the one being worn on a hook for airing between uses.

- Cull your sleepwear down to a few favourites, send the rest to charity and rotate the ones you wear so they all stay fresh and feel nice on the skin.

- If you feel the need to have a couple of sets of sleepwear for travel or for hospital, pop these into zip-lock bags and place them on the bottom of the sleepwear drawer or shelf.

It's a cover up

Organise your outerwear:

- Wire hangers get entangled and are notorious for causing hanger stretch marks! Use a uniform set of good quality hangers, in one colour, to give your wardrobe an instant lift. A good, solid, general purpose, plastic hanger is great for hanging most items such as T-shirts, shirts, tight knits, light jackets and dresses — but not trousers. The weight of trousers is usually too much for the strength of the middle bar on a typical plastic hanger and it will end up bowing. This causes your trousers to wrinkle at the fold, making them unsuitable to wear until you iron out the wrinkles.

- Face items in one direction for easy selection.

- Coats, jackets and raincoats should be hung on heavy-duty suit hangers and covered, when out of season, to protect them from shoulder dust and fading.

- Hang skirts on skirt hangers, one skirt per hanger.

- Hang trousers on skirt hangers, trouser clamps or trouser hangers, and only one item per hanger.

- Jeans and shorts can be hung, or folded and placed on a shelf.

- Shirts and blouses should have the top button done up to prevent them from slipping off the hangers and to keep collars and shoulders straight and in line.

- Eveningwear should be folded and boxed to keep it from sagging, catching, fading and getting dusty and dirty. Wrap it in tissue, place it in a box and store it on a top shelf.

- Loose, textured garments or items with beading, such as tops or dresses, hang out of shape and should be folded on shelves or placed in boxes to protect them.

- Allow breathing space between garments. Only one item should be hung on a hanger — don't double up!

Kick up your heels

Organise your footwear:

- Shoes can be stored in a variety of ways: on shelves or in drawers, heel to heel, toe to heel and one in front of the other. Each has its own advantages. Heel to heel lets you see both shoes facing the front or the back, heel to toe gives you a little bit of extra space where needed. One in front of the other works for deep shelves: you select the one in the front and reach behind for its mate.

- Shoes can go on shoe rails or racks, in wall cupboards, in drawers or on hanging shelving.

- Store boots in boot boxes on shelves and keep them in shape with rolled-up newspaper stuffed inside them.

- If you have lots of sports shoes and minimal storage, place them in a container and store them on shelves.

Dress it up

Organise your accessories:

- Good handbags usually come with bags to store them in. Store them in the bags, label them with the bag's description and place them on a shelf. Stuff bags with newspaper if they need some support to keep their shape.

- Roll scarves up and place them in containers in a drawer or hang them through hoops. Try using multi-level trouser hangers to hang lots of scarves without taking up much space.

- Belts can be hung from hooks on the sides of cupboards or you can purchase special-purpose belt holders. They may also be rolled up and placed in shallow drawers.

- Watches and jewellery can be stored in shallow drawers fitted with jewellery dividers, in hanging jewellery organisers or in fishing tackle boxes. Try putting your earrings in ice-cube trays — they work really well. Of course, there are lots of special-purpose jewellery organisers, boxes and rolls that you can use.

- Noticeboards with hooks can work really well for hanging necklaces.

Tuck me in

Organise your linen items:

- Store sheet sets in their pillowcases on shelves.

- Towels should be folded with the fold facing the front.

- Extra bedding not currently in use can be placed in vacuum bags to reduce the amount of space required. Place it on top shelves until needed.

- Bed and bath linen is often stored in bedrooms to free up space elsewhere or just to have items close to where they are being used.

 Step 6: activ8

Finish it all off and put everything in its place:

- Give the bedroom a thorough clean, including light fittings. Your bedroom should look like the ones you admire in magazines: fresh, clean and welcoming.

- Place items into their new locations, adjusting and adding storage if necessary. Label containers.

- Decide how much you want to have out on surfaces. Aim for the least amount possible. Items on bedroom surfaces take up valuable working space.

- Lastly, add a few decorator accessories to give the room your personal touch.

 Step 7: evalu8

Well done—you've finished the 'Do it' phase! You can now stand back and admire your results and measure them against your vision and the goals you set for yourself. It's time to get your camera out to take your 'after' photos. Compare them with your 'before' photos. *Wow!* What a difference! Go back to the notes you took in the 'Plan it' phase and note your answers to the following questions.

Note it!

✓ Have your frequent frustrations been addressed?

✓ Have you achieved your vision and your goals?

✓ Does your bedroom physically, functionally and emotionally please you?

If you say 'no' to any of these questions, make adjustments now or make a note to follow up within seven days. Continue to evaluate your bedroom and make changes as your lifestyle and circumstances change.

 **Step 8: celebr8**

No bedroom is going to keep itself looking the way yours does right now. You need to add regular bedroom cleaning and maintenance to your home care schedule. So let's quickly make a list of the tasks that need to be done to keep your bedroom humming. Here is an example of timely tasks for bedrooms. Use this list in table 6.1 or create your own.

Table 6.1: timely tasks for bedrooms

Daily	Weekly	Monthly	Quarterly
Make bed like a five-star hotel	Vacuum or wash floors	Clean windows	Tidy wardrobe and de-clutter cupboards
Remove clutter	Dust surfaces and mirrors	Clean bedroom cupboards	Clean blinds or curtains
Hang clothes or take to laundry	Change bed linen	Rotate mattress	Refresh bedroom with a new look and feel

Lock it in!

Once you have completed your own task list, add the tasks to your home care schedule. You will need to lock in a time to complete each task to maintain your new-look bedroom.

Raise the bar!

It's time to set new standards, new rules and new rituals to maintain your clean, organised and functional bedroom.

Keep your 'before' and 'after' photos handy to remind yourself of how far you have come and to see the new standard you have set. Create a few new rules such as: 'I never leave dirty cups and glasses on the bedside table', 'I make my bed as in a five-star hotel' and 'I do an in8minute tidy-up every morning before leaving the room'.

String a few tasks together to create a few new rituals. Your bedtime bedroom ritual could be something like this:

- Set the timer and, in8minutes or less, make bed, put clothing away and clear any clutter.

- Take dirty washing to the laundry.

I bet you will have time to spare!

Create new rituals to guide you through holiday preparation and packing, and any other stressful time periods or tasks.

Maintain it!

Now all you need to do is follow your home care schedule and live up to your new standards. It will be easy to achieve with your fresh, clean bedroom as your foundation.

Congratulations! It's time to celebrate. You did it! You have created a bedroom that is clean, organised and functional. It's time to collect your reward for completing this room. Book in a massage, have coffee with friends, go to a show or just have a bath! You deserve it!

Are you ready for another room? Then turn the page and motor on!

Chapter 7

Fresh faces for living spaces

Children always know when company is in the
living room—they can hear their mother
laughing at their father's jokes.

Anon

Let me entertain you

'We're having a party. Are you coming?'

'I can't wait to get home to snuggle up under a blanket and watch a movie. Hey, where's the remote control?'

'Come on in. Dinner's nearly ready!'

All these questions and statements refer to the day-to-day activities that take place in our living spaces: family rooms, living rooms, dining rooms, billiard rooms, games rooms, rumpus rooms and entrances. They have many names, but they are all living spaces. They bring people together for relaxation and recreation, fun and games, wining and dining, and parties and entertaining. These spaces are also public places. This means that they are often not as disorganised as other areas of the home, due to the occasional frenzied clean-up they receive at the approach of visitors! Together we'll create clean, organised and functional living spaces that you'll be proud to share with your family and friends.

Now read on and I'll reveal the in8steps system checklist for creating fresh faces for your living spaces. Remember to refer back to the in8steps at a glance on page 62–65.

Before you begin

First, let's create a permanent home for all remote controls and TV guides. A basket, container or drawer can serve this purpose, as long as it's a dedicated place and will be used consistently, at least by you. Let other family members know, but until you find a way to totally control other family members, be content with knowing you have a place and that you, at least, will be using it. The others will follow along eventually if you go about it without being a boss or a martyr. Put the remote controls back into their new home, cheerfully and repeatedly, until the family gets the message. Don't nag, boss or tell. Don't even give them the 'look'. Just lead by example. Remember that this journey is about you and your stuff and that being organised is a gift to yourself.

Now clear all surfaces that can be used as sorting areas. Once that's done, grab your notebook and let's get started!

 # Step 1: initi8

Note your frequent frustrations. Does continually searching for the remote controls drive you crazy? Is the furniture littered with old newspapers and magazines? Are you embarrassed to invite friends over for a drink? Do you have so many ornaments that you can't cope with the dusting? It's time to give each living space a fresh face.

Set your vision and your goals, gather your tools and get in the mood.

 # Step 2: investig8

Physically, living spaces are the most spacious areas of the home. They are filled with furniture, bookcases, sofas, cupboards, tables, chairs, rugs, lamps and entertainment equipment such as TVs and sound systems. Books, videos, CDs, DVDs, games and ornaments complete the picture. They often hold all the 'good' stuff: the good china, the good glassware and the good cutlery for guests. Their relative size sometimes attracts items that don't belong in them, just because of the availability of space—especially in corners where a junk pile is sometimes forced to wear a tablecloth so it can pretend it's a piece of furniture!

Functionally, living spaces focus on leisure and celebrations. They bring people together for relaxation and recreation, fun and games, wining and dining, and parties and entertaining. People spend time in living spaces studying, doing homework, listening to music, pursuing hobbies, doing crafts, exercising, watching movies and TV, writing letters or simply dozing off. They are sometimes used as guest rooms when friends sleep over after a late night. And there is more — too much to list. But you get the picture: lots of activities are undertaken in living spaces, so you need to consider them all.

Emotionally, living spaces put on the public face of the home. You want this room to feel and look good for family and friends. Use colour, lighting, furnishings and decorator items to express those feelings.

Step 3: consolid8

Sort your living-space items into big fat categories. Lay out your sorting containers or use surfaces to group items together, throwing out as much as possible along the way. Here is a list of typical living spaces big fat categories with their subcategories. Use them or create your own:

- *entertainment:* games, movies, music, remote controls and TV guides

- *reading:* magazines, articles, newspapers, catalogues and books

- *entertaining:* crockery, cutlery, glassware, platters and vases

- *photos:* prints, negatives, albums and digital photos on media storage devices

- *hobbies and crafts:* stamp collecting, coin collecting, photography, sewing, knitting and scrapbooking

- *collections:* spoons, ornaments and general collectables

- *children's toys:* games, puzzles, building blocks, dolls and trucks

- *transit items:* keys, glasses, handbags, wallets, mobile phones, coats, hats, umbrellas, shoes and schoolbags.

Do it Step 4: elimin8

Eliminate as much as you can by asking the following critical questions of each item you are unsure about:

- Do I use you? If so, how often? When was the last time? When will be the next time?

- Do I need you? Could I use something else as a substitute, or borrow you?

- Do I really want you or just the memory of you or where you came from? To preserve the memory, take a photo!

- Do I love you? Are you of sufficient sentimental value for me to keep?

Set limits on what will be stored in primary and secondary storage space and how much you want in secondary storage space elsewhere. How many CDs, DVDs, books and toys are enough? Consider the amount of storage you have and the users of the living space.

Do it Step 5: alloc8

Allocate containers and locations for what you are keeping. The advantage now is that you can see exactly how much stuff and space you have. The trick is to match the stuff with the space.

Organise your living space by allocating space by person, by function (such as game playing, reading or entertaining), or by type or shape of item (such as crockery, glassware, books or games). The choice is yours, and you can combine them. Do whatever makes sense to you.

Diana's dining dilemma

For the last year Diana's dining room was totally covered in photos, craft paper, ribbons, tools, albums, scissors and cutters. It looked more like a disorganised scrapbooking shop than a dining room in a home. It was time to face her dining dilemma, reclaim the space and entertain again! Diana realised that while her hall closet was rarely used for coats, it would make a perfect craft storage solution. She set about sorting all her craft components and worked out that with the addition of six shelves and an assortment of containers she could customise the closet to accommodate her every craft and scrapbooking need. With her dining dilemma solved, she knew she could invite friends over without compromising her love for scrapbooking and her crafts. With the hall closet conversion nearby, the dining room could now be used for both crafting and entertaining!

Storage smarts for living spaces

Refer to masterclass 4: getting a handle on hardware for a quick refresher, if necessary. When organising living spaces consider the amount of storage space you have and your priorities.

Here are some guidelines for living-space storage.

The games people play

Let's look at how to organise your entertainment items.

Movies

- Movies with covers can be stored by title or by type — for example, children's movies, thrillers, comedies or documentaries. You can number them and create an index so you can easily find the title you want. Store them on shelves or in containers on shelves, with the spines facing out for easy identification.

■ There are many storage units available for movies and the type you use will depend on décor, space, preferences, quantity and frequency of use. Store frequently used DVDs — for example, an exercise DVD you use every morning or your children's favourite movies — in primary storage, and less frequently used ones in secondary storage.

Music
■ Music in all forms can be organised by genre or artist, depending on your preference.

■ Arrange your CDs in boxes on shelves.

■ If you load your CDs onto your current electronic music device, you can release the originals for others to enjoy, while still enjoying the music yourself. If you decide you prefer to keep the original CDs of the music that you downloaded, store your collection in secondary storage, as they will most likely not be accessed very often.

Remote controls and TV guides
■ Have one dedicated location for remote controls and the TV guide. It could be a dish, a basket, a box or a tray — just as long as it fits your remote controls and TV guide and is easily accessible.

■ Encourage everyone to use the dedicated location and at the end of the day pack any strays away.

Turn over a new leaf!
To organise your reading material you will need to have a location where you can store it as well as a place where you can read it. You can set up a reading area by choosing your

favourite chair and throwing in a rug if you like to curl up nice and cosy. Add extra lighting if necessary and have a table or piece of furniture by one side to hold your reading material, your glasses and a snack.

Now that you have your reading station all organised, let's organise the reading material.

Magazines
- Start by looking at all the types of magazines you collect. Categorise them as best you can. Then decide on how many issues you want in primary space and how many issues you might like to keep in secondary storage for reference. If you collect magazines based on your family's hobbies or interests, you might like to have six months in primary space and maybe the rest in secondary storage to free up primary space. The important thing is to set your limits by number, date or the space you want your magazines to occupy.

- Magazines are best stored in labelled magazine boxes. Choose boxes that suit your décor if they are on display.

- Keep the latest edition on a coffee table or by your reading station so you remember to read it.

- If you prefer to keep the article, then experiment with using display books to hold your various collections: one for home decorator ideas and another for children's craft ideas, or maybe you prefer to have just one as a general catch-all. The key is having somewhere to put them. Display books keep the articles clean, are easy to flick through and store neatly on shelves or in magazine boxes. Label the spine for easy identification. Once the book is full, use the 'one-in: one-out' technique for keeping your clippings in check (each time you put a new one in, take an old one out).

Newspapers

Newspapers are easy to store because you don't store them. You read them and ship them out! Pick a number and decide how many days' papers you want to keep in your living space. Aim for a low number such as one or two! Then use the 'one-in: one-out' technique to keep newspapers to their set limit. Place them in a basket or magazine holder or on a surface near where papers are read.

Books

■ As books come in many shapes and sizes and cover many topics, they can be stored in a variety of ways, for example by subject, author or height.

■ As a general rule, store tall books on the top and bottom shelves with smaller books in the middle.

Don't toy with me!

Living spaces are often zones for children's paraphernalia, where children can play under the watchful eye of adults nearby.

Organise your toys:

■ The general rule with toys is that the amount of toys children have must not exceed your capacity to store them. Children are often happy playing with anything. Sometimes a few pots and pans, a wooden spoon and a blanket over a table — better known as a secret cave — will entertain them for hours. Don't create a rod for your own back by keeping every toy your children have ever received over their lifetime. Your children get older and they outgrow their toys. Often it's the adults who have difficulty releasing their children's toys. Neither you nor your children will miss them.

- Keep toys together by type, in baskets or containers on shelves or in a cupboard. If you want them to stay that way, you will need to supervise play and packing away until the children get the hang of what goes where. Label the outsides of the boxes with words or pictures, or stick an example of the contents on the outsides for children to see: a block could go on the outside of the block box, a small doll on the doll box and a small truck on the truck box.

- Limit the number of items out at any one time. Just pick a number. Insist on packing-up time — maybe an in8minutes run-around a few times a day. Rotate toys when boredom sets in for you or the children!

- Toy mats can work well as you just need to pick up the mat and the toys are gathered up!

- Keep puzzle parts together by assigning each puzzle a colour. Simply upturn the puzzle, get a coloured marker pen and run the pen across the back of each puzzle piece as well as the backing board. Store each puzzle's pieces in a zip-lock bag and place it in a box. Keep the backing boards nearby. If two puzzles get mixed up, just turn the pieces over and separate them by colour.

 # Step 6: activ8

Finish it all off and put everything in its place:

- Give the living space a thorough clean, including light fittings. Your living space should look like the ones you admire in magazines: fresh, clean and welcoming.

- Place items in their new locations, adjusting and adding storage if necessary. Label containers.

- Decide how much you want to have out on surfaces. Aim for the least amount possible.

- Lastly, add a few decorator accessories to give the room your personal touch.

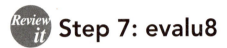 **Step 7: evalu8**

Well done—you've finished the 'Do it' phase! You can now stand back and admire your results and measure them against your vision and the goals you set for yourself. It's time to get your camera out to take your 'after' photos. Compare them with your 'before' photos. *Wow!* What a difference!

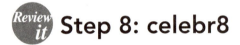 **Step 8: celebr8**

No living space is going to keep itself looking the way yours does right now. You need to add regular living-space cleaning and maintenance to your home care schedule. So let's quickly make a list of the tasks that need to be done to keep your living space humming. Use this list of timely tasks for living spaces in table 7.1 or create your own.

Table 7.1: timely tasks for living spaces

Daily	Weekly	Monthly	Quarterly
Put remote controls away	Dust surfaces	Clean cushions and throw rugs	Tidy and de-clutter cupboards
Clear clutter	Clean ornaments	Vacuum or clean upholstery	Clean blinds or curtains
Hang coats, hats and handbags	Vacuum and Wash floors	Clean windows	Refresh with a new look and feel

Lock it in!

Once you have completed your own task list, add the tasks to your home care schedule. You will need to lock in a time to complete each task to maintain your new-look living space.

Raise the bar!

It's time to set new standards, new rules and new rituals to maintain your clean, organised and functional living space.

Your evening living space ritual could be something like this:

- Do a quick tidy up: put reading material away and shoes away.

- Wash cups and glasses, put reading glasses away, and put phones back on their rechargers.

Ahhh, a calm room to come in to, instead of a chaotic room to avoid!

Create new rituals to guide you through parties and entertaining and any other stressful time periods or tasks.

Maintain it!

Now all you need to do is follow your home care schedule and live up to your new standards. It will be easy to achieve with your fresh, clean living space as your foundation.

Congratulations! It's time to celebrate. You did it! You have created a living space that is clean, organised and functional. It's time to collect your reward for completing this room. Book in a massage, have coffee with friends, go to a show or just have a bath! You deserve it!